The Industrial REVOLUTION

by Randi Reisfeld

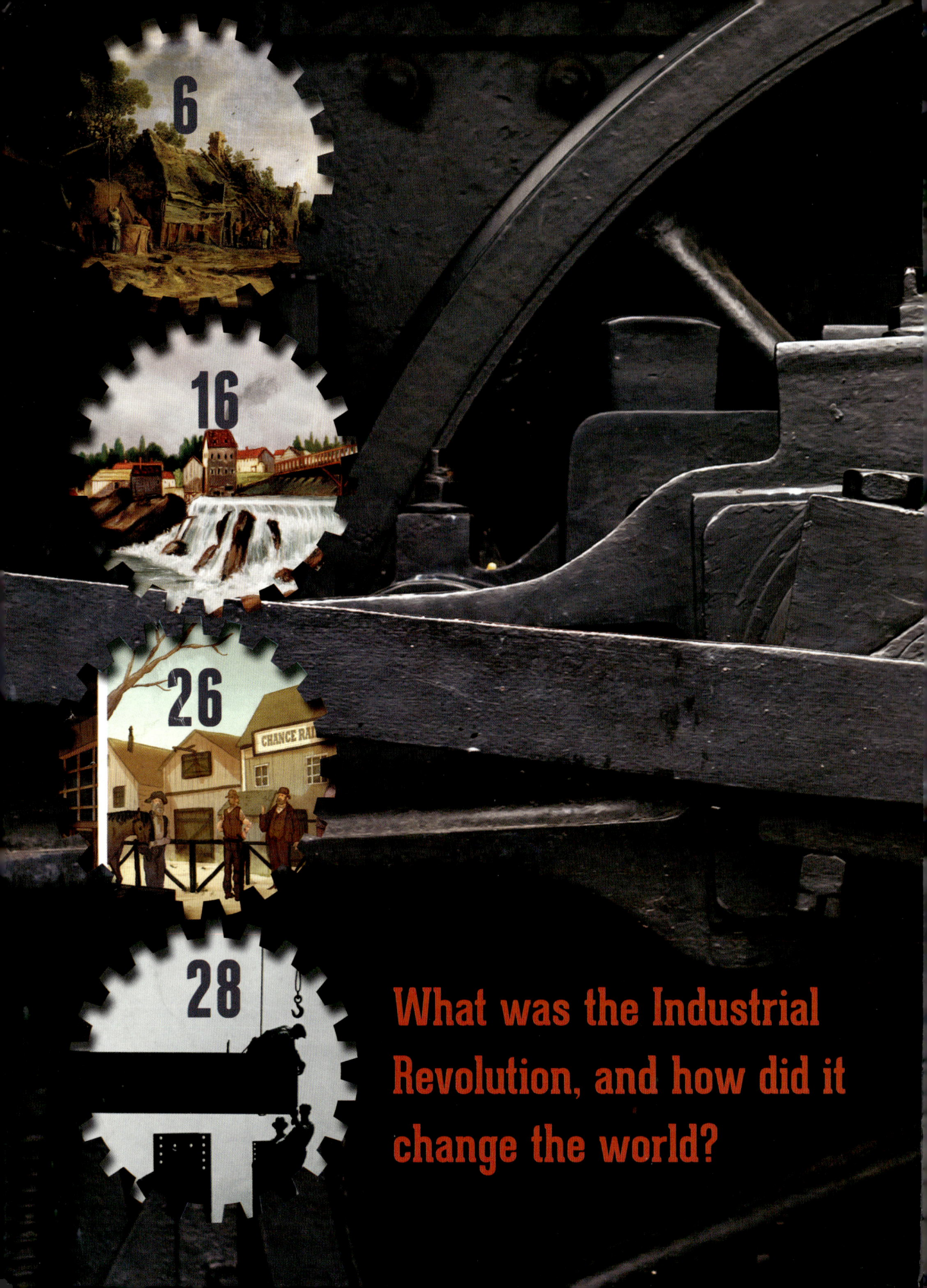

What was the Industrial Revolution, and how did it change the world?

Table of
CONTENTS

MADE to LAST

Prior to the 1880s, the average person typically owned a single pair of shoes. That is because shoes were made one at a time, by hand, by skilled tradespeople. Cordwainers, as they were called, used wooden or stone molds called "lasts" of an individual's foot to custom-tailor every pair of shoes, making shoes expensive to purchase.

▲ Jan Ernst Matzeliger

Then, in the late nineteenth century, Jan Ernst Matzeliger revolutionized the way shoes were made. As a young man in Dutch Guiana (now Suriname), Matzeliger had apprenticed in a machine shop. He became a merchant seaman in order to see the world and settled in America in the 1870s. After struggling to learn the language and gain acceptance, he found work in Lynn, Massachusetts, at a shoe factory and learned the cordwainery trade. He observed that the shoe-making process was hindered by lack of mechanization. In particular, the last step, which involved the fitting and nailing of the leather upper over the sole of the shoe, was extremely time-consuming. In 1883, after several years of testing different models, he patented his designs for a "shoe-lasting machine."

19th Century

Prior to the Industrial Age, shoes were custom-made by a local craftperson who used a template of the consumer's actual foot to fit and form the shoe.

20th Century

Innovations such as the lasting machine and assembly lines revolutionized the shoe industry.

21st Century

Today, a great majority of the shoes purchased in the United States are manufactured overseas.

Before that, it took one skilled shoemaker ten hours to complete 50 shoes by hand. Using the shoe-lasting machine, a less-skilled worker could complete up to 700 shoes in a day, increasing production more than tenfold.

Because more shoes could be completed in less time, the cost of making a shoe decreased by up to 50 percent and the supply increased. Following the law of supply and demand, more output meant that shoe prices decreased. Shoes were now more affordable for most people.

The shoe-lasting machine is an example of industrialization, when manufacturing technology enables businesses to mass-produce, or make large quantities of a product. Mass production allows cuts in manufacturing costs, provides a steady supply for the market, and therefore lowers the price, making it more affordable to consumers.

Beginning in the 1750s and spanning all the way until World War I, major changes in technology and manufacturing practices brought about an Industrial Revolution in many parts of the world. Historians generally divide the Industrial Revolution into two major phases: the First Industrial Revolution (1760s–1840s) and, with the advent of new steelmaking processes, the Second Industrial Revolution (1850–1910s). During this time, inventions such as the lasting machine and countless other innovations replaced work previously done by hand. The result was a social and economic transformation that impacted the lives of generations of people and changed the course of history. It also came with a high price tag. Today technology continues to change daily life at lightning speed, but what were the early technological breakthroughs that ushered in the modern era? Read on to find out.

Rise of the MACHINES

ESSENTIAL VOCABULARY

- abundant   page 14
- agrarian   page 7
- fossil fuel   page 14
- industrialization page 13
- scarce   page 14
- steam engine   page 13
- textile   page 9
- turbine   page 13

Farms once used common land, but then landlords used fences to enclose their properties and keep commoners from using those lands.

▲ The manor, where the landlord lived, was the heart of the feudal system.

What key factors helped bring about the First Industrial Revolution?

Although there is no exact date marking the start of the Industrial Revolution, historians agree that there is a place where it all began. The seeds of change of the First Industrial Revolution first rooted in Great Britain, the one-time ruler of the United States.

Prior to the 1800s, Britain, like most of Europe, was rural. More than 90 percent of the population lived in the countryside or in small villages. Britain was an **agrarian** society, in which agriculture was the predominant way of life. Most people were farmers who grew their own food, raised their own livestock, built their own homes, and made their own clothes. In other words, people relied on themselves and the land to meet their basic needs. Farmers and local craftspeople used simple tools. The most cutting-edge technology at the time was the horse-drawn iron plow invented in 1730 by Joseph Foljambe.

For centuries, some farmland was considered common land. Peasants could use it to hunt and let their livestock graze. But beginning in the sixteenth century and continuing to the nineteenth, landowners got Parliament to pass a series of laws called the Enclosure Acts. These laws allowed landlords to fence off their lands. The fences kept the peasants off the former common lands, thereby depriving them of a way to make a living. Thus, the enclosure movement created a class of landless workers, many of whom left the countryside and moved to cities in search of work. The creation of this class of available workers created a labor force that would be a critical factor in making the Industrial Revolution possible.

THE ROOT OF THE MEANING

The term **commoners** originally referred to farmers who worked on common land. It comes from the Latin word *communis,* which means "public, shared by all or many." Now the term refers to those whose family are not descended from nobility.

The Dawn of Factories

Beginning in the early 1700s the Industrial Revolution began in Great Britain. One way to understand the Industrial Revolution is to think of it in four simple steps.

1

Inventors and scientists developed and built machines capable of performing tasks previously done by hand.

2

Manufacturers bought the machines and built factories to house them.

3

Factories were built alongside rivers, where waterpower was used to run the machines. Workers were needed to run these machines.

4

Landless farmers looking for jobs that paid a decent wage moved to towns or cities to work in these factories.

CHECKPOINT

Visualize It

What was rural life like before the Industrial Revolution in Britain?

With its steady supply of new workers, resources, inventions, and access to the Thames River, London was one of the first cities to become industrialized.

Soon places such as London, Manchester, and Liverpool—all British cities with rivers at their center—became home to factories that held the machines that would change the world. The shift from agricultural to industrial society had begun.

The **textile** industry, where cotton or wool fibers were spun into thread or yarn and then woven into cloth, was the first to undergo a major change. The wool came from British sheep farms, and the cotton came from the Americas and, later, from India.

But before the invention of advanced spinning machines, the creation of yarn was a time-consuming process done by farming families in their home, or cottage. The term *cottage industry* comes from this old practice.

New inventions, such as the spinning mule, which was able to spin cotton thread much faster than any one person, helped to bring textile production out of people's homes and into large factories. Textile manufacturers built factories, also called mills, in the cities to house the new inventions. With water from rivers providing the energy to power the machines, mills sprang up throughout England.

▲ **British factories relied heavily on raw materials from the Americas.**

Inside the textile mills, the owners broke down the process into separate tasks. Some workers might be in charge of carding the fiber, some would spin thread or yarn, and others would weave the thread or yarn into fabric. John Kay invented the flying shuttle in 1733. This mechanized loom allowed weavers to weave fabrics both wider and faster. It was so effective that it used up thread faster than it could be spun, exceeding the capacity of spinners at the time and placing spun thread in constant shortage. Since spinning fiber into thread or yarn was always the longest, most painstaking part of the process, many inventors tried to find a solution.

The Spinning Jenny

The spinning jenny, which improved upon such simple tools as the spinning wheel, was one of the first machines that moved Britain forward into the Industrial Revolution. It was invented by carpenter and weaver James Hargreaves in 1764. The idea was patented in 1770. Hargreaves's spinning jenny made it possible for a single worker to spin ten times as much thread by hand.

The Water Frame

The spinning jenny was followed in 1769 by Richard Arkwright's spinning frame, which came to be known as the water frame because it was powered by waterwheels. This machine was the first automatic textile machine. It allowed an unskilled worker to spin many threads simultaneously. Because it was too large to fit in a home and instead required a factory space, the machine helped transform spinning and weaving from a cottage industry to a factory production. Arkwright's mill in Derbyshire, England, was also the first mill to employ a continuous process from raw cotton to finished product.

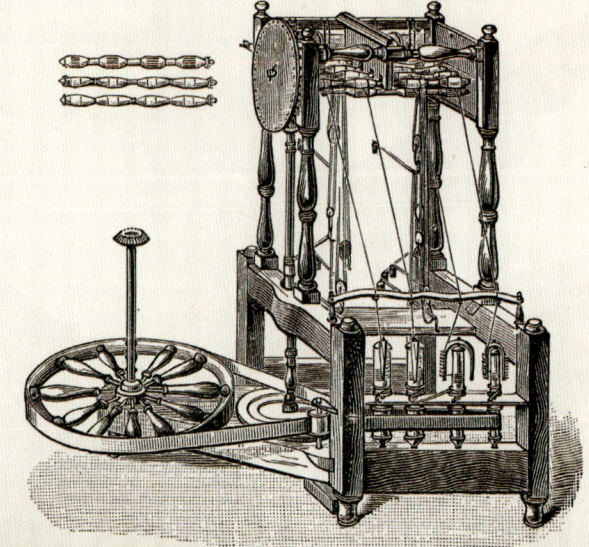

Working with a power loom was often dangerous and required the user to be extremely careful.

The Spinning Mule

Shortly thereafter, in the 1770s, Samuel Crompton improved on these inventions when he crossed the spinning jenny with the water frame and invented the spinning mule. His invention also was powered by water, but it spun strong, thin thread up to one thousand times faster than by hand, increasing spinning capacity and the demand for raw materials.

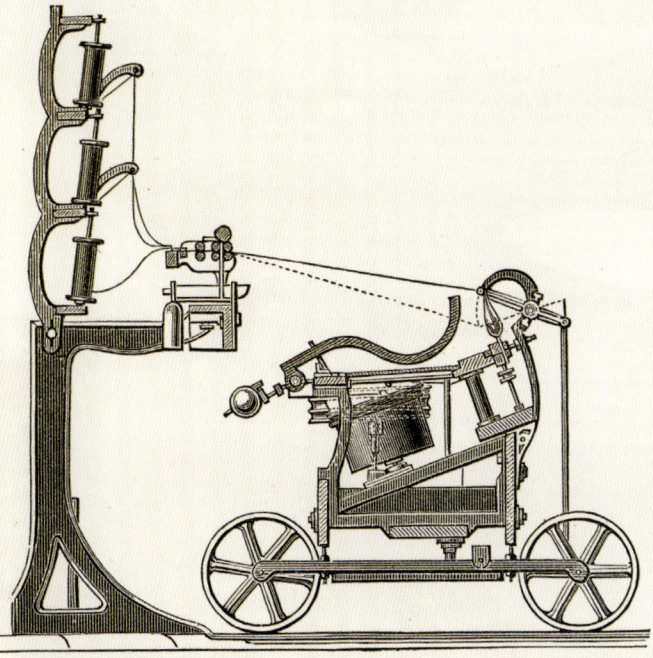

The Power Loom

Up until this time, much of the factory-spun yarn was still being woven at home by master weavers. Then, in 1784, Edmund Cartwright invented the first power loom. This steam-powered machine mimicked the movements of the weaver and wove thread and yarn into textiles forty times faster than a hand loom.

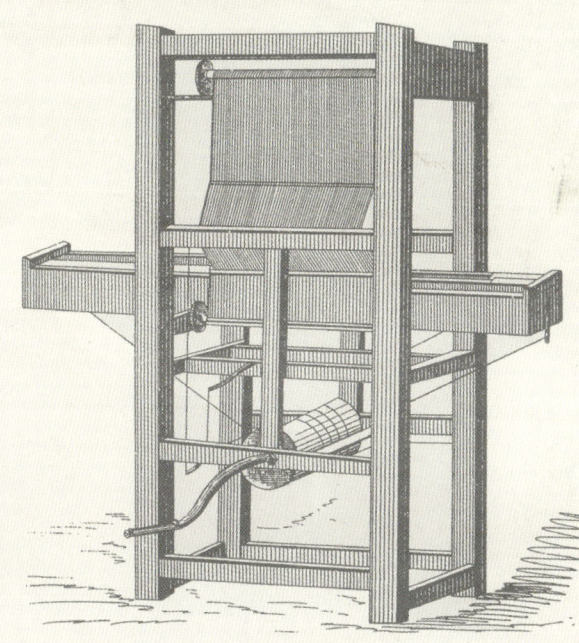

11

The Steam Engine

Early mills ran almost entirely on waterpower. The steady flow of water that surged from swiftly rushing rivers provided kinetic energy that turned waterwheels and kept mill machines and factories running efficiently. The advantage of water as a power source was that it was steady and dependable. The disadvantage was that rivers were not portable. They could not be moved to another location. Early factories had to be built directly along the water source.

Beginning in the late 1600s, British inventors had experimented with machines that were powered by steam. In 1698, Thomas Savery invented a steam-powered water pump. He believed that an engine like his could be used in mills that were not near rivers. In 1712, Thomas Newcomen improved on Savery's invention. He built a steam-powered water pump that was used to drain accumulating water from mines. Both machines were inefficient, however, and were never widely used.

HISTORY AND SCIENCE

How Steam Engines Work

In a steam engine, a liquid (usually water) is pumped in and heated in a wood- or coal-fired boiler. The boiler rapidly increases the temperature, and the water becomes highly pressurized. The steam moves the blades of the turbine in the same way that wind moves the blades of a windmill. Those turbine blades then move cranks or wheels to convert the steam energy into useful work.

In 1765, Scottish inventor James Watt created a new and improved **steam engine**. His engine used the steam from boiling water to turn a **turbine** and generate energy. His invention also had two separate containers to keep steam hot for a longer period of time. It was more powerful and efficient than any attempts that had come before. The new rotary steam engine finally allowed factories and mills to be built anywhere, regardless of river access. Watt's rotary steam engine provided the power behind **industrialization** in Great Britain and other parts of the world.

▼ The invention of the steam engine allowed industry to rely on energy sources other than water and wind power.

THEY MADE A DIFFERENCE

James Watt (1736–1819)

Even as a child, James Watt liked to invent things. Growing up in Scotland, he built models with the tools in his father's workshop. Watt began his career as a maker of compasses, scales, and other mechanical instruments. In 1764, he turned his attention to improving the steam engine. By 1790, his invention had made him a wealthy and respected man who forever changed the world. Watt is sometimes called the Father of the Industrial Revolution.

▲ In honor of his work, the scientific unit of measurement for power, the watt, is named after him.

Raw Materials

By the late 1700s, the demand for steam power grew and with it the demand for a fuel source that could heat water to generate steam energy. At first, wood was burned. When forests were cleared and wood became **scarce**, coal became the solution. Coal is a nonrenewable **fossil fuel** that was plentiful in Britain and the United States. Unlike wood, coal was slow-burning, which made it a more efficient fuel source. Coal also was **abundant**, but, it was not as easily extracted from Earth. Coal had to be mined, which meant digging deep underground. Mining was extremely perilous work. Miners were exposed to toxic gas emitted from Earth while digging. Mines also had structural problems that often resulted in collapse, trapping and killing miners.

As the steam engine and mechanical inventions increased the speed of manufacturing and transporting goods, the demand for the raw materials to make goods also increased. England's growing textile industry increased the demand for raw cotton, which in turn meant that more cotton crops had to be grown every year. As a result, the American South needed more land to grow cotton and more enslaved laborers to harvest and process that cotton so it could be shipped across the Atlantic. Soon textile mills began popping up in the American Northeast— the demand for cotton would skyrocket.

▲ The Industrial Revolution began with the textile industry and made cotton an increasingly hot commodity for the coming centuries.

HISTORY AND ECONOMICS

The Law of Supply and Demand

The law of supply and demand is an economic principle related to the price of raw materials or goods. According to this law, the value and price of a commodity— something that is grown or mined such as cotton or coal—or finished goods, such as textiles, will increase with demand. The greater the demand, the greater the price. The lower the demand, the lower the price.

Coal is still used to produce electricity and heat throughout the world.

Summing Up

- Industrial growth started slowly, beginning in Great Britain in the 1700s, because that country had access to waterpower, raw materials, and available workers.

- The Industrial Revolution changed where people lived.

- The textile industry was the first to benefit from industrialization.

- Improvements made to the steam engine led to industrialization, which began to spread around the world.

PUTTING IT ALL TOGETHER

Choose one of the following research activities. Work independently, in pairs, or in small groups. Share your responses with your class and listen to others present their work.

1 The Industrial Revolution can be defined as: things formerly made by hand in the home now being made by machines in the factory. Research various goods and make a list of examples from the early years of the Industrial Revolution. Of these, which one do you think was the most important? Then explain how this change impacted the price of manufactured goods and also the way people lived their lives.

2 Pretend you are leaving your farm to go to work in a factory for the first time. Write a diary entry explaining what you might see or feel as you take your first walk through a busy, industrialized city. Compare the city with the farm you've just left.

3 Research an inventor from the Industrial Revolution. Learn how this person came up with his or her most important invention. What problem was that person trying to solve with the invention? Make a model or a diagram explaining how the invention worked, and describe its social and economic impact.

CHAPTER 2

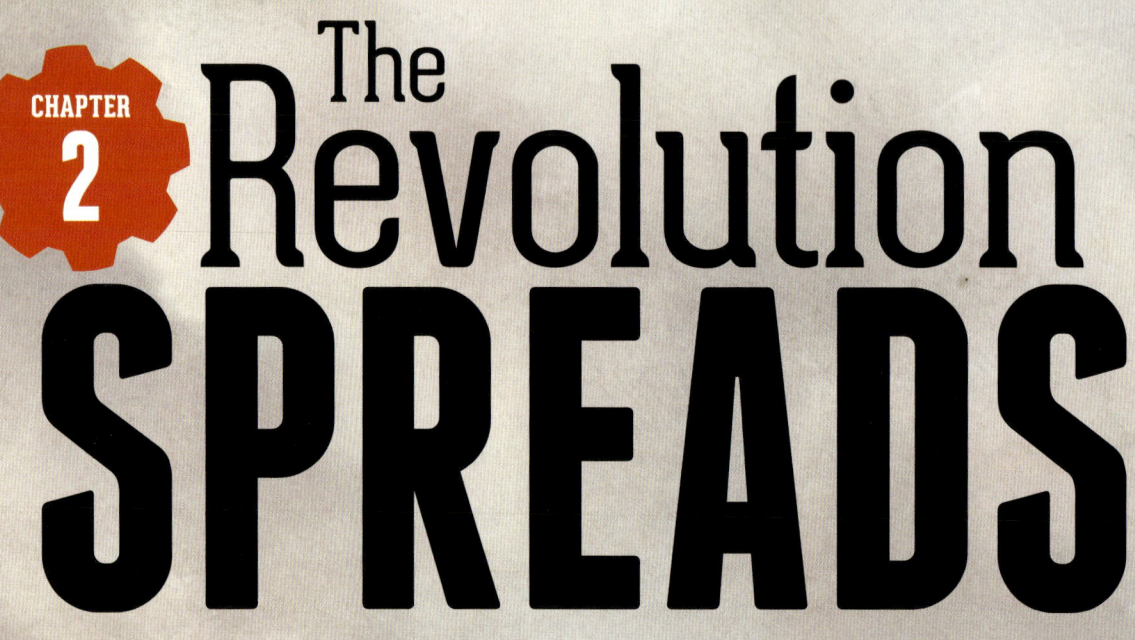

The Revolution SPREADS

ESSENTIAL VOCABULARY

- barge page 20
- canal page 20
- emigration page 24
- famine page 24
- immigration page 24

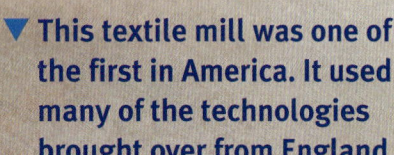

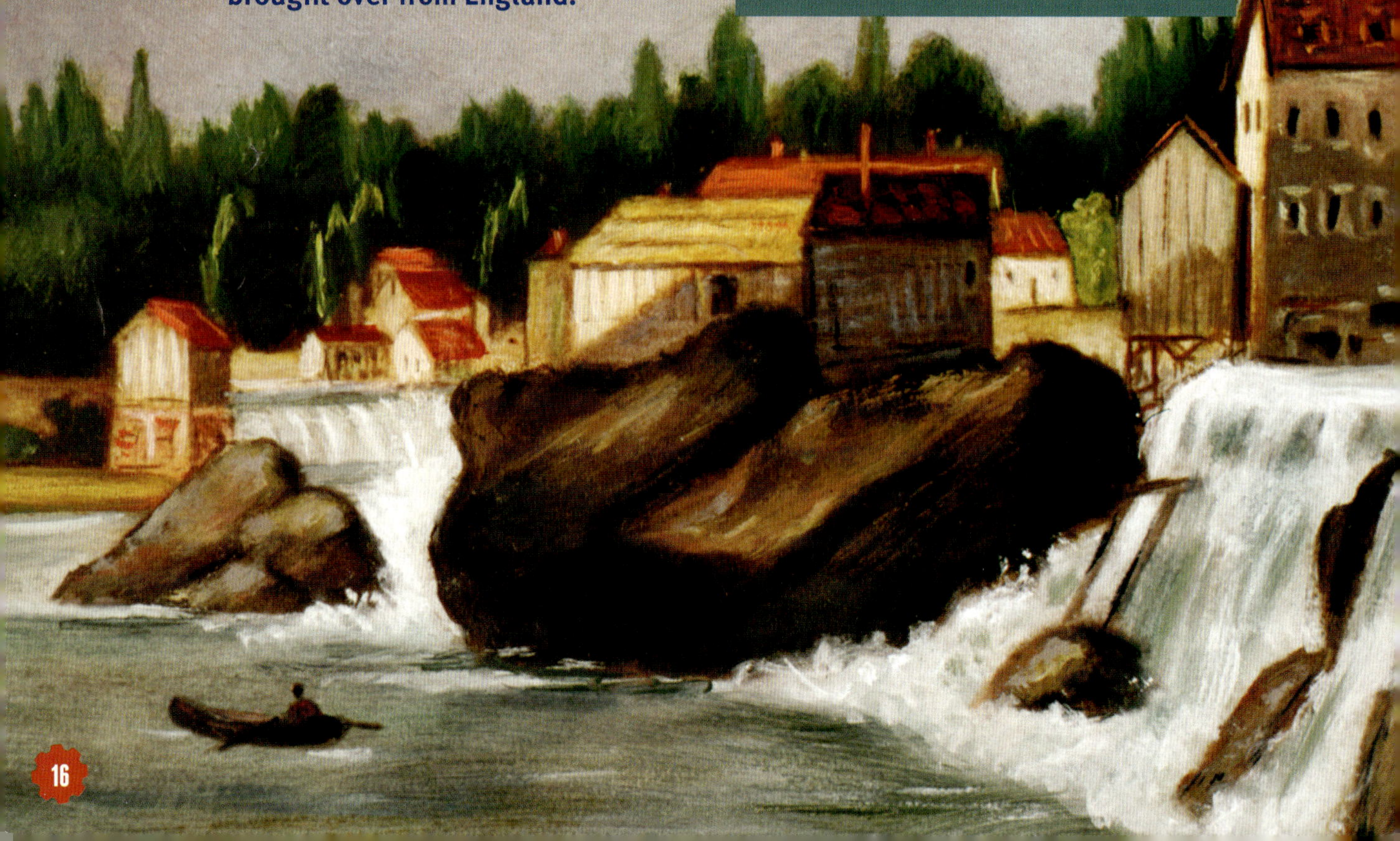

▼ This textile mill was one of the first in America. It used many of the technologies brought over from England.

How did the Industrial Revolution take shape in the United States?

British industrialists would have loved to keep their technological secrets to themselves. They were having tremendous success importing raw materials from the Americas, using these resources to make goods in their factories, and then selling the new products around the world. However, Americans were quick to see the advantage of industrialization. It improved lives and created wealth, especially for manufacturers. Within a decade after the American Revolution, as the United States began to establish itself as an independent nation, it began to industrialize.

Industry Comes to America

In 1789, British mill operator Samuel Slater came to America, and in 1793 he opened the first American textile mill, in Pawtucket, Rhode Island. America was in an excellent position to industrialize. The country was expansive, its land rich in untapped raw materials and natural resources. Like Great Britain, the United States had plenty of wood and coal as well as waterways to power factories and mills. There was also a strong population of workers.

Americans were also resourceful. It was not long before Americans used and improved on the British machines already in existence and invented new machines. The Northeast was the center of the Industrial Revolution in the United States. Cities in Massachusetts, Rhode Island, Connecticut, New Hampshire, New York, and New Jersey had been centers of business, trade, and government since the very first days of the American colonies. These states bordered the Atlantic Ocean and had access to major rivers and waterways, making them the first to industrialize.

While Sam Slater's contribution was critical, the United States had many homegrown inventors to rival those in England and other parts of the world. Among them was Eli Whitney, whose "cotton gin" helped transform the American economy. As a child, Whitney was a creative and resourceful boy who made and sold hat pins and other small inventions. After studying at Yale College, Whitney went to work as a tutor on a Georgia cotton plantation and quickly observed the difficulties of processing cotton. Separating the seeds from the cotton fibers was a laborious task that took hours to complete.

In an effort to solve this problem, Whitney developed a machine that removed the seeds from cotton, a process traditionally done by hand. The cotton gin had a wooden drum with wire hooks that pulled

cotton fibers through a wire screen. In 1794, he patented his new machine, the cotton gin. In the past, it could take a laborer an entire day to clean about half a kilogram (1 pound) of cotton. Using Whitney's cotton gin, that same laborer could process up to 25 kilograms (55 pounds) of cotton daily.

The cotton gin allowed southern growers to process and supply more cotton to meet the demand of northern mills. Southern states thrived as the demand for their cotton crops increased. The employment of mechanical looms also allowed fabric and textiles to be woven faster, further

▼ **In 1794, Eli Whitney was granted the patent for the cotton gin.**

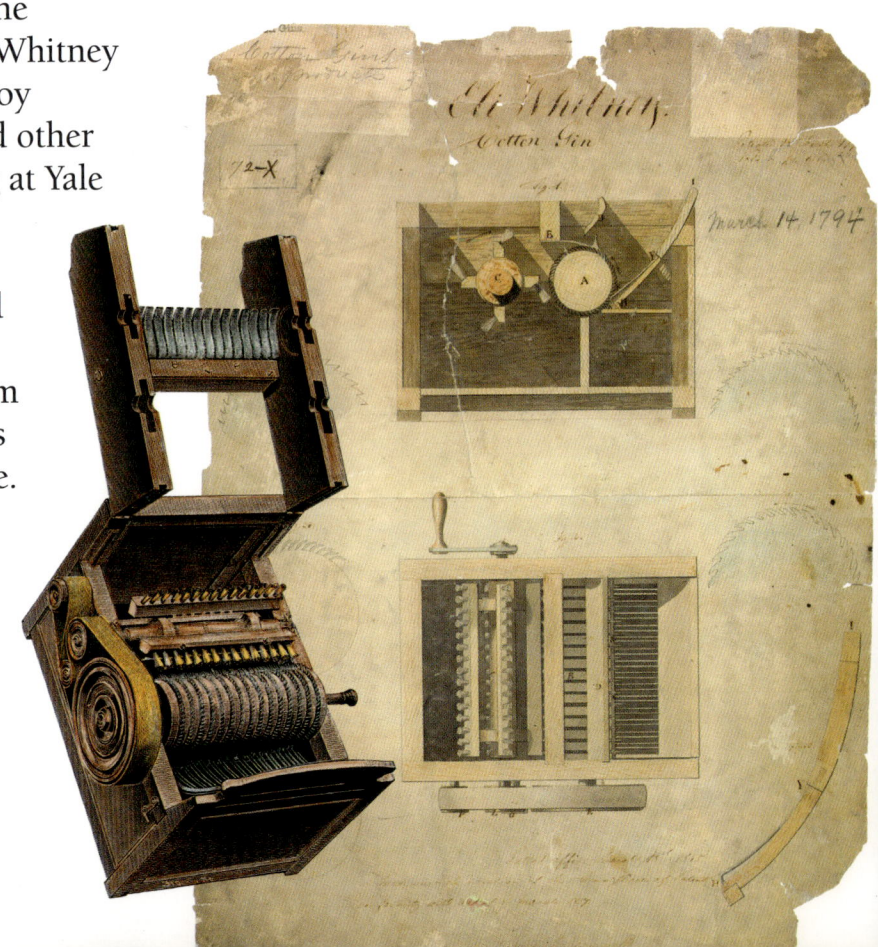

Eli Whitney

boomed in industrial cities. New York City and cities in New Jersey saw tremendous growth thanks to the impressive textile mills that surged with power and produced high-quality goods. Many cities in the northern part of the United States remained textile centers for decades, until they were replaced by cities in the South. Today many American textile plants have moved to other countries, where fabric is produced even faster and less expensively.

THE ROOT OF THE MEANING

The term **gin**, as in cotton gin, comes from the word *engine,* which came to mean "mechanical device" in the 1200s. In Old French, *engin* means "skill, cleverness." The term originated in Latin as *ingenium,* which means "inborn qualities or talent."

increasing the demand for cotton. Since plantation owners could make such high profits using enslaved labor, they wanted to grow more cotton, and for that, they needed more land. Soon cotton began to replace other crops and became the major cash crop of the South.

Meanwhile, Northern states prospered as textile mills there churned out cloth made from woven cotton. Since many more workers were needed to staff the factories, the population

GEOGRAPHY AND TECHNOLOGY

Paterson, New Jersey: "Silk City"

The city of Paterson, New Jersey, was founded in 1792 to serve as an industrial city. The site was chosen because of its location near the powerful Great Falls, rugged cliffs that dropped water 23 meters (77 feet) into the Passaic River. In its earliest years, Paterson was home to dozens of mills and factories that utilized the falls for power, but the product that made Paterson famous was silk. Textile mills produced this luxury fabric, which is spun from fibers made by silkworms—the larvae caterpillars of the silkworm moth. In the late 1800s and early 1900s, Paterson exported so much silk it was nicknamed Silk City.

Transportation: Waterways

At the start of the Industrial Revolution, manufacturers needed to find better, faster ways to transport raw materials and equipment to the factories and deliver new goods to market. In the eighteenth century, roads were narrow and unpaved. They were dusty and dry in the summer, and in the spring and winter they were wet and muddy. The wheels of horse-drawn carriages or stagecoaches sometimes got stuck along the flooded roadways.

One solution to the slow roads was the construction of **canals**. These artificial rivers began as simple trenches filled with water. Later, the canals were more carefully constructed, using locks to climb hills. Some connected to lakes,

rivers, or oceans, while others connected one city to another. Canals provided a way to transport goods by **barge**, a long, flat-bottomed boat used to carry freight on rivers and canals.

In the United States, the biggest canal was the Erie Canal. Construction began in 1817; eight years later, the Erie Canal was open to trade and travel. The canal connected the Great Lakes to New York City, making it an international trade destination. The canal greatly decreased the cost of shipping goods throughout the region. Most importantly, it opened up a huge new territory in western New York and western Pennsylvania and allowed for settlements in states such as Ohio and Illinois.

▼ **Canals were a major source of transportation in many U.S. cities.**

Railroads

Canals turned out to be a good solution to the transportation problem brought about by the need to connect raw materials with factories. Manufacturers soon, however, discovered a better way to transport goods and people: the steam railway locomotive and the railroad. In the mid-1800s, the building of railways began to boom and would soon spread to all continents.

Like many inventions, the railroad was the result of the work of several engineers and inventors. Building a railroad also took many years of hard work to construct. As the years went on, innovations were developed to improve on the systems already in place.

The new railroads made use of the steam engine. English mining engineer and inventor Richard Trevithick brought steam power to rail travel. Trevithick built the first full-scale working steam locomotive. It made its first journey on February 21, 1804, hauling a train full of iron from the Penydarren Ironworks in Wales and replacing a team of horses that had previously done this job.

In 1830, Robert Stephenson, an English civil engineer and the son of a man who built locomotives, improved on Trevithick's ideas. His *Planet* locomotive had its wheel axles on the inside rather than the outside of the wheel. This design kept the locomotive more streamlined and increased speed and efficiency.

▼ **Railroads transported goods and people from the East Coast to the West Coast of the United States.**

Thanks to more efficient use of iron and steel, railroads soon became the safest, fastest way to travel. In the United States in 1869, locomotives from the Central Pacific and Union Pacific railroad companies met at Promontory Summit, Utah Territory. There, a golden spike was driven into the tracks, linking the West Coast to the East Coast by rail. This first transcontinental railroad bound the country together as nothing else before. By 1876, a trip from New York City to San Francisco, which used to take months by stagecoach or weeks by ship, could now be completed in five days. The opportunity to settle vast new territories proved irresistible to millions of Americans.

Railroads did more than connect the country. New cities sprang up along the railway lines. By the beginning of the 1900s, long trains brought raw materials across miles of track to new industrial centers, such as Pittsburgh, Pennsylvania, which became the home of the steel industry, and Birmingham, Alabama.

◀ **The Stourbridge Lion was built in England in 1828 and transported to the United States, where it was the first locomotive seen in the country.**

CHECKPOINT

Ask Questions

Research the concept of time zones. Why were they created?

Pioneers of Industrial Technology

Several inventors made contributions by creating and applying new inventions in different ways.

Samuel F. B. Morse

Prior to 1837, all news, messages, and letters were transported via horseback, boat, or train. It could be weeks or even months before a letter was received. Then, in 1836, the artist Samuel F. B. Morse and others began to develop an electrical telegraph system to devise a much faster and more practical way to transmit information. Its basic components were a battery, an electromagnet, and an electric switch known as a key, with a metal plate beneath it. When the key came into contact with the metal plate, it made a clicking sound. To make use of the new system, Morse devised a code for sending and receiving signals over a distance. Known as "Morse code," it consisted of "short" clicks and "long" clicks, also known as dots and dashes. It was a new kind of alphabet. With the code, words and full sentences could be exchanged over long distances.

Henry Bessemer and William Kelly

In 1856 another major innovation was called the Bessemer process. Henry Bessemer, an Englishman, and an American named William Kelly discovered a new way to super-heat iron, turning it into steel. Steel was a stronger metal than iron, and once their process went into use in factories, steel could be produced faster and at a lesser cost; it therefore became less expensive. Now railway tracks, bridges, and tall buildings could be made using stronger steel rails and girders. Steel would also be used to create stronger machines and more powerful weaponry.

By increasing the speed of communication from months to minutes, the telegraph forever changed the way ordinary people, military operatives, and businesses communicated. ▶

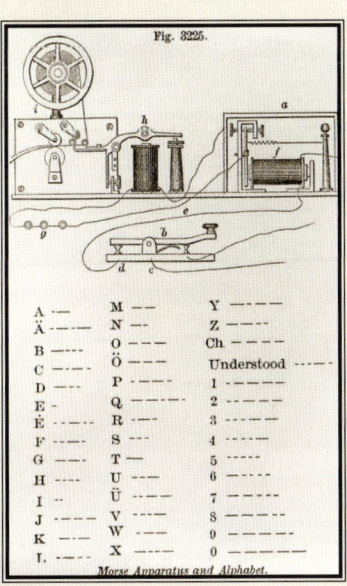

▲ Bessemer and Kelly patented identical steelmaking processes. After Bessemer bought Kelly's patent, the process became known as the Bessemer process.

Immigration and the Industrial Revolution

Throughout the 1800s, the United States saw a massive growth in population in big industrialized cities. This was in great part due to the **emigration** of millions of people leaving other countries to find a better life in America. The movement of people into a country is called **immigration.**

Millions of immigrants came, most of them making the voyage by steamships. Many of the earliest immigrants were German, Irish, and British. A large number of them were fleeing from the poorest of living conditions. Beginning in 1845, for example, the Irish potato **famine** caused the destruction of Ireland's potato crops. One million people there died of starvation. Another million emigrated, mostly to America.

Others came to find political and religious freedom. They were not allowed to practice their religions in their native countries. Jews were discriminated against in parts of Russia and Poland and came to America to escape the pogroms in eastern Europe. A wave of German political refugees fled to America after the failed 1848 revolutions.

Immigrants worked long hours, were poorly paid, and suffered from discrimination. Still, life in the United States was often better than the lives they had left behind.

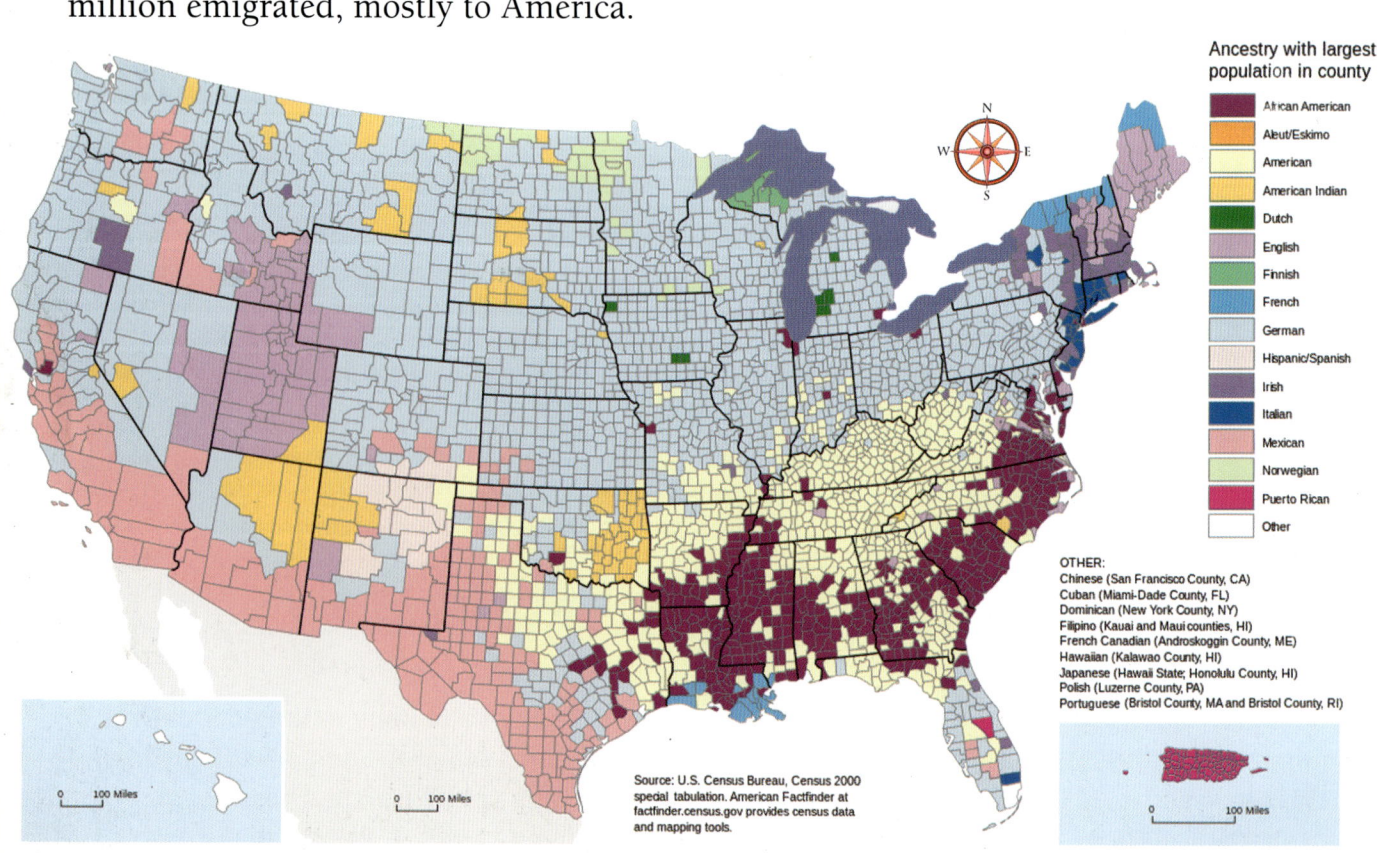

Ancestry with largest population in county

African American
Aleut/Eskimo
American
American Indian
Dutch
English
Finnish
French
German
Hispanic/Spanish
Irish
Italian
Mexican
Norwegian
Puerto Rican
Other

OTHER:
Chinese (San Francisco County, CA)
Cuban (Miami-Dade County, FL)
Dominican (New York County, NY)
Filipino (Kauai and Maui counties, HI)
French Canadian (Androscoggin County, ME)
Hawaiian (Kalawao County, HI)
Japanese (Hawaii State; Honolulu County, HI)
Polish (Luzerne County, PA)
Portuguese (Bristol County, MA and Bristol County, RI)

0   100 Miles

0   100 Miles

Source: U.S. Census Bureau, Census 2000 special tabulation. American Factfinder at factfinder.census.gov provides census data and mapping tools.

0   100 Miles

Summing Up

- When the Industrial Revolution came to the United States, many important inventions and improvements, such as the cotton gin, canals, and railroads, were created. Many were built on previous advances.

- Iron, coal, and steel advanced the progress of industrialization.

- More jobs were available, and the increase in immigration supplied people to fill them. Immigrants moved from their homelands to cities in order to find new opportunities in factories there.

PUTTING IT ALL TOGETHER

Choose one of the following research activities. Work independently, in pairs, or in small groups. Share your responses with your class and listen to others present their work.

1 Create an Invention Hall of Fame with your classmates. Working alone or in pairs, select an inventor/innovator from this period and create a plaque honoring this person's contribution to industrial progress. State why this person should be included in the Invention Hall of Fame. Each plaque should contain a picture of and accurate historical information about your selection.

2 Before trains and canals, people and goods could not travel as quickly or efficiently. Create an advertisement for a new train line or a canal, explaining the benefits of these technologies.

3 Learn and use Morse code. Conduct research to learn how to write and read the telegraph code. Then use Morse code to communicate a "secret message" to your classmates that includes letters and numbers. First record it on paper; then knock out the Morse code on your desk or some other hard surface, with your hand or a ruler. Finally, write a short reflection on what you learned from the activity.

PROFIT OR LOYALTY?

CARTOONIST'S NOTEBOOK BY DENIS O'ROURKE AND HEIDI WARD
ILLUSTRATED BY ALEX CAÑAS

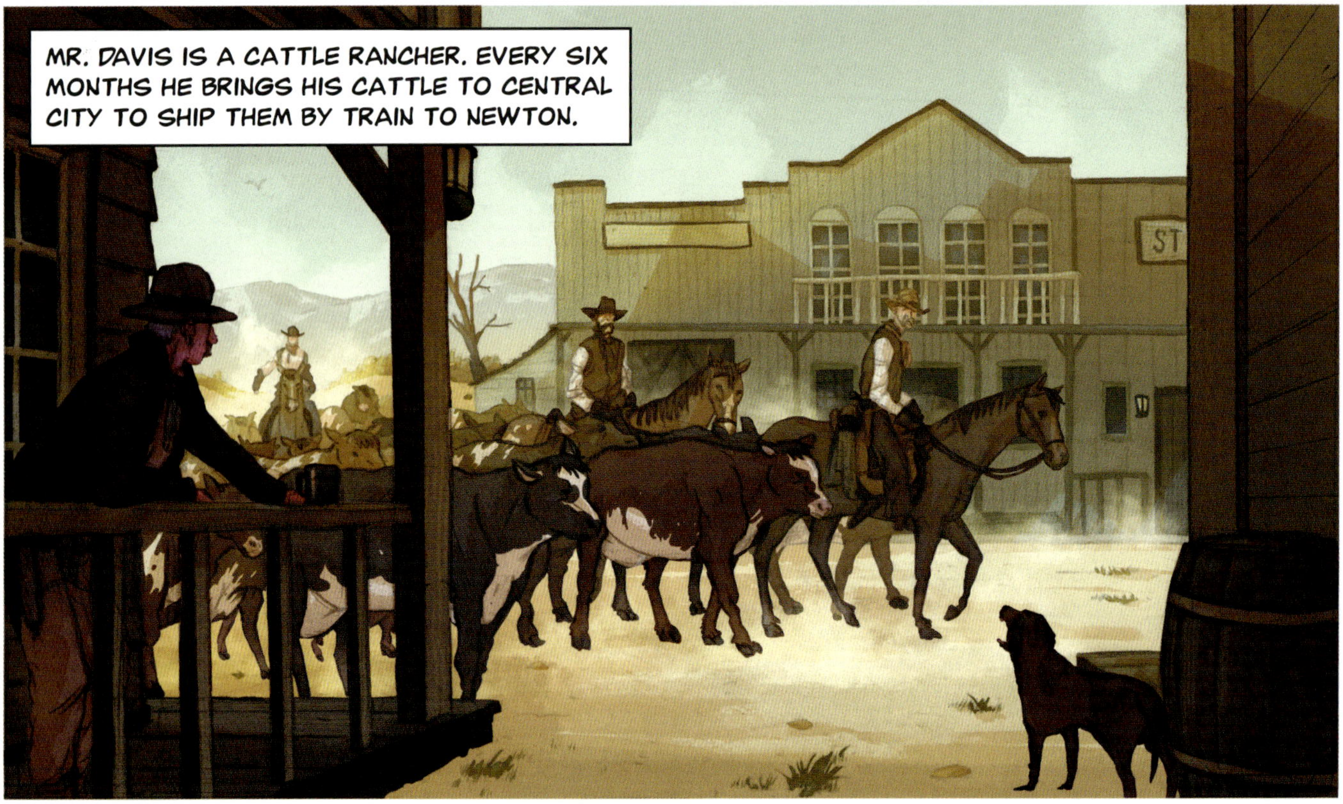

TWO RAILROAD LINES CONNECT THE TOWNS OF CENTRAL CITY AND NEWTON, WHICH ARE 200 MILES APART. THE RAILROADS ARE OWNED BY MR. NORTH AND MR. CHANCE.

MR. DAVIS IS A CATTLE RANCHER. EVERY SIX MONTHS HE BRINGS HIS CATTLE TO CENTRAL CITY TO SHIP THEM BY TRAIN TO NEWTON.

FOR YEARS MR. DAVIS HAS USED THE RAILROAD OF HIS TRUSTED FRIEND, MR. NORTH.

BUT NOW MR. CHANCE WAS OFFERING A CHEAPER RATE.

SEVENTY-FIVE CENTS PER ANIMAL.

WHAT SHOULD MR. DAVIS DO? SHOULD HE SAVE MONEY BY SHIPPING HIS CATTLE WITH MR. CHANCE AND POSSIBLY CONTRIBUTING TO THE FORMATION OF A MONOPOLY? OR SHOULD HE PAY EXTRA AND CONTINUE TO SUPPORT HIS FRIEND MR. NORTH? EXPLAIN YOUR ANSWER.

THE SECOND
Industrial Revolution

The increased availability and affordability of steel building materials launched the Second Industrial Revolution.

What were the major effects of the Second Industrial Revolution?

The Bessemer steelmaking process of 1856 ushered in the second phase of industrialization, called the Second Industrial Revolution. During this time, the money people earned by working in a factory, textile mill, or manufacturing plant was a vast improvement over what they could make by farming or doing most other types of work. Those who immigrated to the United States coveted factory jobs as a way to earn a good and respectable living for themselves and their families. They were able to pay for housing and other basic necessities—with a few dollars left over for some luxuries.

Some former farmers found that factory work was less physically strenuous than farmwork. Another advantage was that they no longer had to worry about weather ruining crops. Factory work, however, did have its share of difficulties. Employees often worked in filthy conditions for long hours. The machines could be dangerous, and it was not unusual for a worker to be seriously injured or even killed on the job. As a result, the need for workplace reform became more and more obvious. Some workers asked their employers to put safety regulations into place. At first, however, most did not.

Progressive Reform

To improve their working conditions, some employees tried to organize into groups called unions. A **union** is a group of workers who join together to advance their interests through collective bargaining. Unions gave workers more power and a way to demand both reforms in the workplace and higher wages. If the union's demands were ignored, sometimes members banded together and refused to work by going on **strike**.

Without workers, factories could not operate. Owners lost income immediately. While some of the early union strikes were successful, many more were not. It was not unusual for factory owners to send people into the factory to break up the strike. Other employers simply replaced strikers by hiring other, more desperate laborers to fulfill the disputed jobs.

Child labor was a cruel fact of life during the Industrial Revolution.

Child Labor

Beginning with the first textile mills, children ages 7 to 12 were employed as factory workers. They were put to work running sewing machines and other equipment, as well as in mines, where small bodies or hands were useful. Although needy parents most often sent their older children to work, it was not against the law for children as young as 6 to spend as much as sixteen hours a day in factories. Children were the most prone to serious accidents on factory floors.

The United States wasn't the first newly industrialized country to face these struggles. Britain already had dealt with many of the same issues. In the 1800s, the British government passed a series of laws called the Factory Acts. These laws required better pay and safer working conditions for workers. Some later laws also limited the number of hours a child could legally work. Some U.S. factories saw the benefits of keeping their workers safe, and they too began

THEY MADE A DIFFERENCE

Jacob Riis [1849–1914]

Jacob Riis (pronounced Reece), a reporter for the *New York Tribune*, took pictures of the slums of New York City and put them together in an 1890 book titled *How The Other Half Lives*. His gritty photographs brought attention to the lives of tenement dwellers and helped spur early social change.

▲ Jacob Riis's photographs opened a nation's eyes to the suffering in the slums in New York City.

to make changes in their work systems. By 1916, U.S. child labor laws were being passed. These kept children under the age of 14 out of most factories and those under 16 out of mines.

Pollution and Poverty

In addition to poor working conditions and child labor, pollution also was a constant problem. The dirt and smoke billowing from factory chimneys shrouded the cities and even clung to curtains hanging inside apartments and houses. Today conditions like that would not be tolerated in the United States and most of Europe and Asia, but in those days few cared. Making money and inventing new ways to do so took precedence.

Breathing bad air paled in comparison with the poverty and overcrowding. As the Industrial Revolution created more jobs, cities became overcrowded and many people could not find decent, affordable housing. Newcomers had to live in boardinghouses. Entire families were forced to live in small rented rooms. Others crowded together in apartments called **tenements**. These tenements often had poor plumbing and lacked fresh air circulation.

Factories created air pollution, pumped out through the smokestacks. Homes heated by coal added to the problem.

As waves of new immigrants arrived, they struggled to assimilate, or fit in, with their new neighbors. Immigrants naturally preferred the safety and familiarity of living near those who had come from their own countries. Soon, ethnic enclaves known as Little Italy and Chinatown sprang up. Most of these neighborhoods were in the poorest, most densely populated sections of the city; however, these areas did foster mutual support organizations, ethnic newspapers, and general fellowship among people sharing common traits.

HISTORY AND LITERATURE

Hard Times

In his 1854 book *Hard Times*, well-known British novelist Charles Dickens (1812–1870) depicted the horrors of industrial life in fictitious "Coketown," a city that was covered in a fog of despair and sadness:

"Seen from a distance, in such weather, Coketown lay shrouded in a haze of its own. You knew the town was there, because you knew there could have been no such sulky blotch upon the prospect without a town."

The Civil War

During the years 1860–1861, the Southern U.S. states **seceded** from the Union and formed their own country, the Confederacy. In an effort to keep the United States as one country and preserve the Union, President Abraham Lincoln declared war on the Confederacy. This was the beginning of the Civil War.

There were several reasons why the Southern states wanted to form their own country. One was the conflict over whether new states forming in the West would be "slave" states or "free states." Another was the issue of tariffs. Manufacturers, who were mostly in the North, wanted high tariffs to make foreign imports more expensive relative to domestic products. Southerners generally wanted low tariffs so the goods they bought from abroad would be less expensive. The Industrial Revolution was another cause of the Civil War.

The Northern states had more than five times as many factories as the Southern states. The North also was home to nine of every ten skilled workers in the country. The North was better able to build railroads, canals, and roads, which made it much easier for businesses to deliver their products to customers.

The Southern states produced most of the cotton as well as other crops utilized by those factories and mills. A textile mill in New England relied on the cotton grown and processed in the South. The economy of the South depended on agriculture. It was a lucrative economy, and many people, especially plantation owners, became wealthy. Unfortunately, the agricultural economy of the South relied primarily on enslaved African American laborers. In the early 1800s, abolitionists in the North began insisting that the Southern states end slavery and free their slaves. To do that, Southerners felt, would cripple their economy.

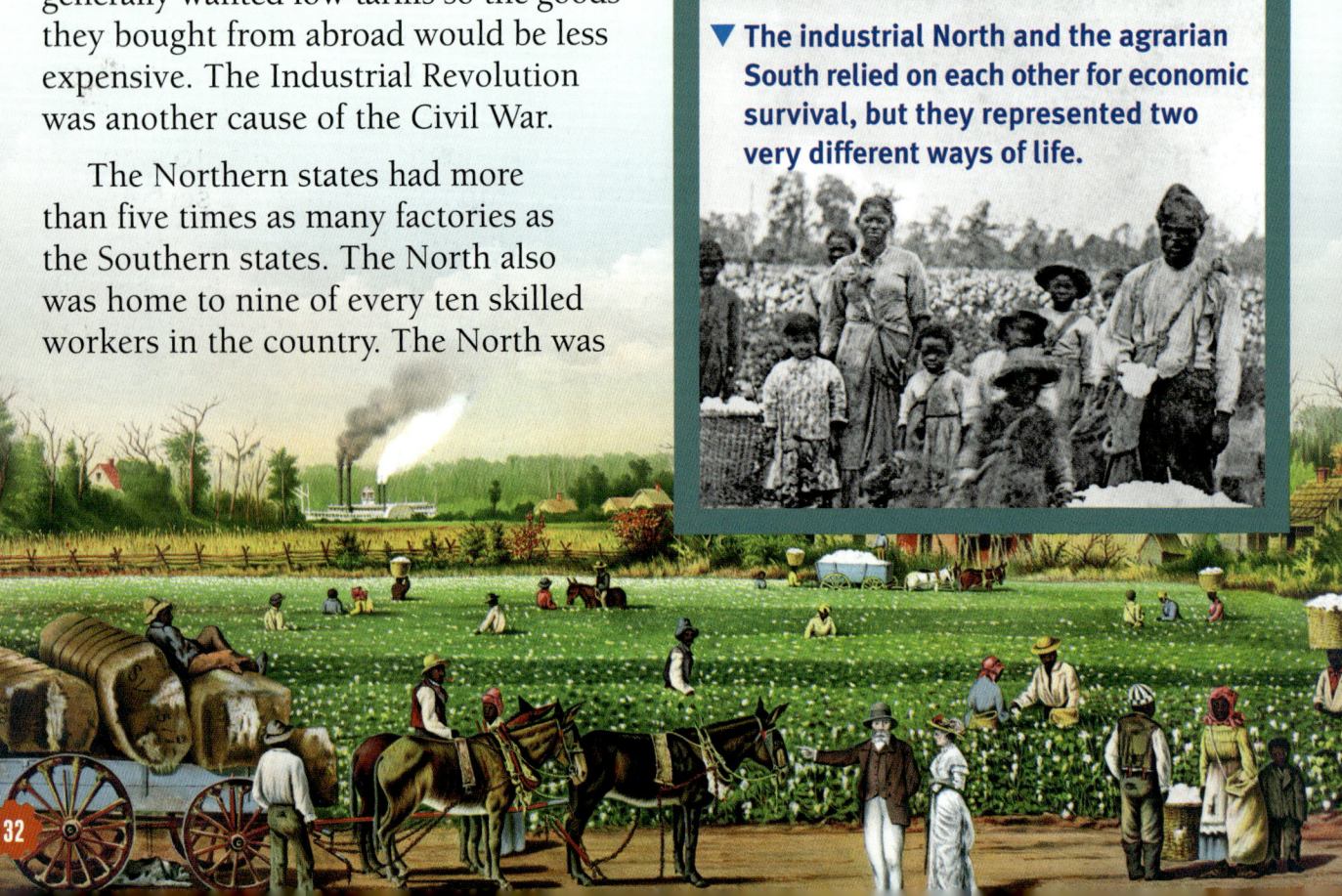

▼ **The industrial North and the agrarian South relied on each other for economic survival, but they represented two very different ways of life.**

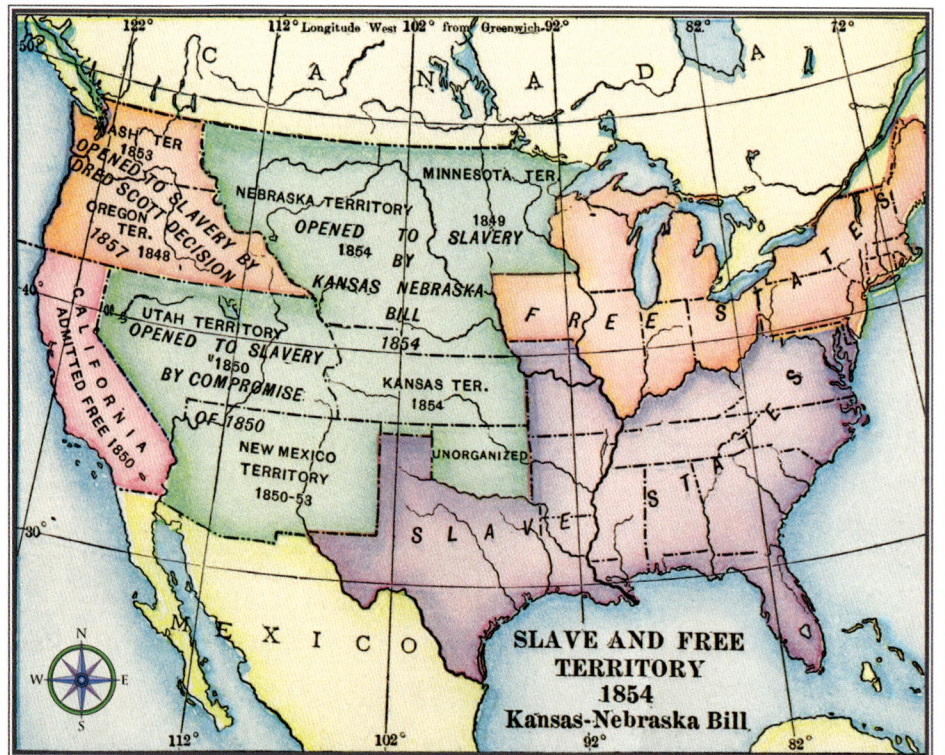

SLAVE AND FREE
TERRITORY
1854
Kansas-Nebraska Bill

CHECKPOINT

Ask Questions

How did the Industrial Revolution impact the outcome of the Civil War?

As the United States grew, the differences between North and South deepened. They fought over new territories, arguing whether new states should be free or slave states. Violent struggles in the new territories soon erupted.

Industry played a major role in the Civil War. The factories of the North produced powerful new cannons and guns that held more ammunition and could kill more soldiers. The weapons could also fire at great distances and were more accurate.

Telegraphs helped both sides. The machines kept information flowing from battle sites to both regions. Railroads played an important role, carrying soldiers and supplies to encampments and battle-torn areas.

The Confederate states were led by excellent generals, such as Robert E. Lee. He and his officers were brilliant tacticians, which meant they could carefully plan battles and make excellent decisions. The Confederacy took the war far into Northern territory, blasting into Gettysburg, Pennsylvania, in 1863. But the North had industrial power and its large population to fight back. Northern factories pumped out machinery, and new immigrants were eager to gain citizenship in exchange for serving in the military. The North had the advantage once the war began to stretch out from weeks and months into years.

In April 1865, General Lee was forced to surrender to the Union general, Ulysses S. Grant, officially ending the war. With the end of the war, both sides were compelled to look at the tremendous losses and damage suffered. The nation would have to rebuild its war-torn lands and the political strength of the Union. The Industrial Revolution made that task easier.

Captains of Industry or Robber Barons?

For many Americans, life during the late 1800s was difficult. The South was rebuilding after the Civil War. Freed slaves often lived in poor conditions, not dissimilar to their former slave quarters. Farmers fought and struggled in the Plains, and urban workers in the East and Midwest were demanding better pay while living in the squalor of tenements.

The Civil War had taken its toll on the United States. The bitter price paid in loss of human life and monetary resources was high for both sides of the conflict. Still, the industrial growth and westward expansion of the United States continued. America's newly **annexed** western territories were rich in resources such as gold, silver, copper, oil, and petroleum. There were also vast stretches of land with fertile soil, perfect for growing such crops as wheat and corn and raising cattle to produce meat and dairy products. These raw material resources helped further industrialization in the United States and abroad.

THEY MADE A DIFFERENCE

Andrew Carnegie (1835–1919)

Born in Scotland, Andrew Carnegie immigrated to the United States with his family when he was a child. Ambitious and driven, he worked his way up from telegraph messenger boy to owning the largest steel mill in the United States, in Homestead, Pennsylvania. Carnegie was a ruthless businessman who did not want to spend money improving safety conditions in his factories. He battled union workers in 1892 at his Homestead Steel Mill. He also used his money and power to close down other businesses that tried to compete with him. His company, Carnegie Steel, was sold to J. P. Morgan in 1901 for $480 million, the equivalent of $14 billion today. Later in life, Carnegie used his money to open libraries, hospitals, and universities. His "Gospel of Wealth" article, printed in the *North American Review* in 1889, urged other wealthy industry owners to be generous and to share their fortune with others.

▲ The steel industry made Andrew Carnegie one of the wealthiest men in the United States.

▲ Political cartoons often have a bias, or a distinct point of view.

Those Americans in a financial position to take advantage of those resources would bring about what Mark Twain referred to as "The Gilded Age," during which the great robber barons amassed their wealth by building **monopolies** in various areas of industry.

Andrew Carnegie made his fortune as the dominating distributor of steel. In 1901, he sold his company, Carnegie Steel, to J. P. Morgan, who also went on to become a multimillionaire. Oil was the source of wealth for others. John D. Rockefeller became the richest man in the world owing to his Standard Oil Company, which controlled 80 percent of the oil refining industry. Cornelius Vanderbilt's wealth was due to his ownership of most of the major railroad networks.

POLITICAL CARTOON

Captains of Industry

Opinions about these wealthy Americans were divided. Many felt they exemplified the American dream: anyone who worked hard could be happy and successful. And with wealth, they could be generous. Stanford University, the J.P. Morgan Library, and Carnegie Hall were all funded by those who became rich during this era. Critics held that many of these industrial millionaires were corrupt, calling them robber barons. Some historians say they grew wealthy from exploiting (mistreating) workers, bribing politicians, and spying on their competitors. They were not afraid to use violence against workers or rivals.

Some of these industrialists used their power to enter politics. Leland Stanford headed a railroad company and served as both a governor of California and a U.S. senator. Stanford sometimes used his political power to protect his business interests.

Major Technological Advances

Telephone Communication

The invention of the telegraph led to an even more revolutionary way to transmit information, one that was eagerly embraced by people around the world. Inventor Alexander Graham Bell built on Morse's idea. In 1876, Bell and his assistant Thomas Watson created what they called "the Speaking Telegraph." Instead of a series of dots, dashes, and long and short clicks that needed to be translated, this new invention, called the telephone, was able to translate human voices into electrical impulses that could be converted back to sound at the other end of a long wire almost instantly. In other words, there was no longer need for a code. By 1886, some 150,000 phones were in use throughout the nation.

▲ Alexander Graham Bell, working with Thomas Watson, is credited with inventing the first telephone.

Electricity

Thomas Edison was perhaps the most well-known inventor of the Second Industrial Revolution. Although he is credited with hundreds of inventions, including the phonograph and the movie camera, he is most famous for his electric lightbulb of 1879. A savvy businessman, Edison started the Edison Illuminating Company to generate direct current (DC) electricity. He also developed research laboratories to find even more uses for electricity. Edison's biggest contribution to the Industrial Revolution was setting up a central electrical generation plant for the distribution of electricity over a grid, or network of wires throughout a city. Variations of this grid are still used today. Edison's greatest rival was the genius Nikola Tesla, who invented a more efficient way of distributing electric power called alternating current (AC) electricity. Working with George Westinghouse, he developed an AC generator that could cover longer distances without losing power.

Edison was also credited with inventing the ▲ first incandescent lightbulb, which had a life of about thirteen hours, long enough to make the lightbulb practical.

Aviation

The late 1800s and early 1900s was a period of great innovation in the transportation industry. On December 17, 1903, two brothers from Dayton, Ohio, did the unthinkable. On the Outer Banks of North Carolina, Orville and Wilbur Wright made aviation history as the first men to fly. They invented the first successful airplane and the first controlled, powered, and heavier-than-air human-piloted aircraft.

The Wright brothers used glider technology and experimental flying research to create aircraft controls and fixed-wing powered flight. The birth of flight meant that people would soon be traveling between distant locations in ever-shorter time.

The first flight of the Wright Brothers' Flyer lasted twelve seconds.

THEY MADE A DIFFERENCE

Henry Ford (1863-1947)

Henry Ford was not an inventor. Instead, Ford was an excellent salesman and industrialist who knew how to make a good product more affordable. In 1908, he introduced a simple, easy-to-operate car called the Model T, which was perfect for families. He used interchangeable parts (a concept developed by Eli Whitney some years earlier). Ford installed an assembly line process in 1913, which increased efficiency. Because Ford believed that his factory workers should be able to afford a Model T, he kept his wages higher than other auto manufacturers and production of the Model T soared. Unlike most industrialists, Henry Ford thought of his workers not only as employees but as consumers, too.

Motorized Transport

Cities themselves were changing. The elevator, invented by Otis Tufts—and more importantly, the elevator brake, invented by Elisha Otis, which made elevators much safer—made a new type of building possible: the skyscraper. Skyscrapers, tall buildings with apartments or offices one atop the other, were made possible because of steel and elevators.

HISTORY AND TECHNOLOGY

The Assembly Line

An assembly line is a manufacturing process in which interchangeable parts are added as a product moves down the line. For example, as a car frame moves down the assembly line to each worker, he or she supplies a needed part. The worker rarely moves—it is the car that moves down the line. With Ford's innovative system, cars that previously needed twelve hours of assembly time could now be complete in about two hours.

▲ Assembly-line workers could produce a car in a short time, making it affordable for the average American.

◀ By today's standards, those first skyscrapers were not very tall, only ten to twenty stories.

Imperialism and Nationalism

The availability of steel and the innovation of the assembly line allowed nations to continually improve and expand. As the nations of Europe became more industrialized, the need for raw materials increased—so they looked abroad. Sometimes they conquered other countries to claim natural resources and control trade. This was called imperialism. **Imperialism** means that one country extends power over other countries to create an empire.

During the mid- to late 1800s, European nations and the United States set out to establish economic control over raw materials found in Africa and Asia by setting up new colonies. By moving into these developing countries, they hoped to build larger markets and increase their wealth. The major nations, including Great Britain, Spain, and Germany, gained a sense of power and importance as their empires grew.

These colonies, largely undeveloped, had no defense. Across the globe, more powerful nations commandeered large areas of land, built factories, and took control of the resources these small countries had to offer.

The Industrial Age also saw the rise of **nationalism**, the spirit of patriotism and unity that people feel about their homeland. Although it sounds like a positive concept, nationalism would eventually lead European nations (and the United States) into two major wars and many smaller ones.

MAP XV.
THE WORLD,
Showing the Colonial Possessions,
By A. von Steinwehr
From Thalheimer's Mediæval and Modern History, by permission.

England & her colonies.
France " "
Portugal " "
Spain " "
Holland " "

World War I

In the early years of the twentieth century, competition between the major industrial nations intensified. Britain, France, and Germany in Europe were joined by the United States, Russia, and Japan as the most powerful industrial nations. Fed by increasing wealth and power, and a sense of fierce nationalism, these nations became suspicious of one another. In 1914, the assassination of Archduke Franz Ferdinand of Austria led to the outbreak of World War I, a devastating conflict often referred to as the "Great War."

During World War I (1914–1918), battle strategies changed tremendously from the wars of earlier years. The Industrial Revolution had resulted in such military innovations as armored tanks, high-powered machine guns, fighter aircraft, and even poison gas.

The advances in technology made the Great War more fierce and bloody than any previous war. The machine gun, for example, accounted for about 80 percent of the casualties in the Great War. Generals relied on trench warfare—the tactic of digging trenches, or ditches where soldiers could hide and shoot at their enemies from a distance. To prevent attacks, armies turned to new weapons such as land mines and barbed-wire mines. These killing machines destroyed lives and tore up miles of land. The devastation throughout Europe was enormous.

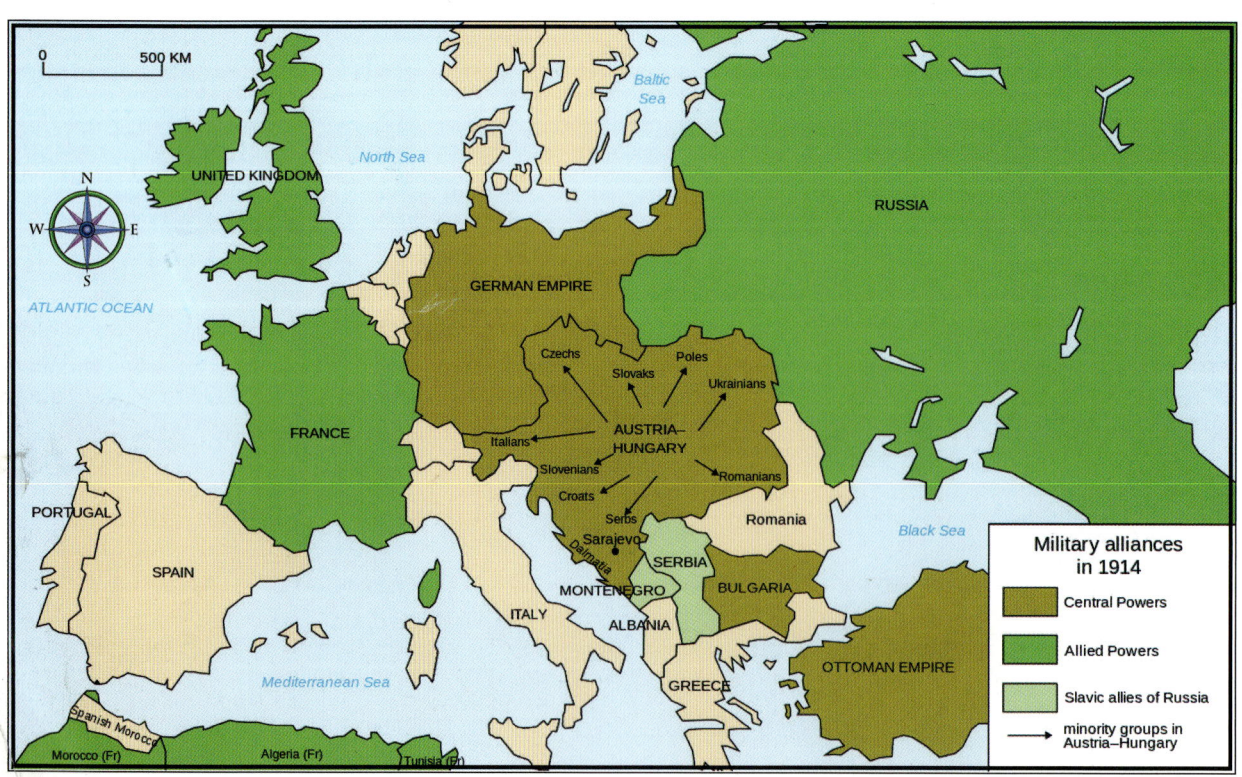

▲ **During World War I, the two sides fighting were the Allied Powers (France, Britain, and Russia, and later the United States) and the Central Powers (Germany, Austria-Hungary, and the Ottoman Empire).**

Summing Up

- In just over one hundred years, the United States went from a collection of farming colonies to an industrial power, unified from coast to coast. New technologies changed the country.

- Some immigrants settled on farms, while others moved to growing cities.

- Travel and trade became easier. Technology brought wealth and power to some but caused hardship for others.

PUTTING IT ALL TOGETHER

Choose one of the following research activities. Work independently, in pairs, or in small groups. Share your responses with your class and listen to others present their work.

1 Plan and create a time line that shows the order of major events in America during the Industrial Revolution.

2 Research and examine photos of child labor taken by Lewis Hine. As if you had lived when the photos were taken, write a letter to the editor of an imaginary local paper protesting this practice. It should include two arguments against child labor.

3 Some men during the Gilded Age were considered either captains of industry or robber barons. Conduct some outside research on John D. Rockefeller, Cornelius Vanderbilt, J. P. Morgan, or someone of your choosing, and write a short biography. Was this person, in your opinion, a captain of industry or a robber baron? Was it possible to be both?

A World CHANGED

The Cuyahoga River, in Cleveland, Ohio, was once so polluted by factory waste that it actually caught on fire. Since the 1970s, efforts have been made to keep the river clean, and national environmental laws began to appear to protect the land and the waterways.

"One never notices what has been done; one can only see what remains to be done."

— Marie Curie, 1894

In 1844, Samuel Morse sent out the first message on his new invention, the telegraph machine. It read: "What hath God wrought?" Like Morse, the great innovators of the Industrial Age were unsure about what kinds of changes new inventions would bring to the world.

For centuries, life had centered around farms and small villages. Across Europe, Asia, Africa, and the Americas, people had their own small societies and traditions that stretched back thousands of years.

Many of the advances that made the Industrial Revolution possible had been around for centuries. People had always been inventing things. But during the Industrial Revolution, the number and speed of new inventions increased greatly.

After the Industrial Revolution, the world was brought closer together. Innovations in transportation made trade and travel fast and inexpensive. New communication technologies, the telegraph, telephone, and radio, would end much of the isolation the world had endured. It was able to lift people out of poverty and create a society where everyone could enjoy inventions and products that had once been available only to the very rich.

Industrialization did not come without a price. For some, that price was devastating. Industrialization, and the jobs it created, resulted in overcrowding in cities, housing shortages, and poor working conditions. New weapons made warfare deadlier, with cannon fire giving way to machine gun bullets and later atomic weapons. Factories led to the exploitation of poor workers in underdeveloped countries and to polluted air, water, and soil. Although many lives have been enriched, poverty and corruption still exist. In some ways, we fight the same battles today as we did hundreds of years ago.

Changing Technology

phonograph

record player

portable cassette player

MP3 player

How to Write an
ARGUMENT

1 Choose a topic that interests you. It should be a topic on which people have differing opinions.

2 Research the topic well. Find evidence and statistics on the topic.

3 Take a position on the topic based on your research.

4 Decide on the format and audience for your argument.

5 Outline your piece of writing.

6 Write a first draft.
Remember a few tips:
a. State your position and present a few strong reasons to support it.
b. Clearly present each reason in a paragraph. Include evidence to support your position.
c. Write a strong conclusion in which you restate your position and offer a solution.

7 Revise and proofread your writing.

The Bakery of the Future Must Invest in Technology

There are real challenges facing Main Street's bakeries. For these mom-and-pop bakeries to stay in business, technology is the answer. For success in an ever-changing marketplace, small retailers must look to the technology used by larger wholesalers in order to continually innovate to stay competitive.

Using the latest technology will allow corner bakeries to reduce overhead costs and increase profits. Mechanized oven technologies and cooling systems can ensure long-term savings by reducing energy costs and eliminating multiple employee salaries. Automation and computerization will also allow these small businesses to streamline inventory control and customer service and allow owners to spend more time and resources on brand building and expanding their customer base and market share.

Investing in the future isn't cheap, but the alternative is certain failure. Local bakeries must embrace technology and work toward the kind of speed and efficiency that will launch them into the twenty-first century. This will allow them to increase customer volume and profits, giving industrial bakeries a run for their money.

Bakeries of the Future Must Look to the Past First

Many local bakeries today are facing extinction due to storefront rent hikes and dwindling downtown foot traffic. The answer, some would have you believe, is technology and all of the cost-cutting measures that innovation and efficiency promise. However, investing money in fancy new computerized ovens and refrigeration and online customer interface is not the way to save America's bakeries.

New equipment is expensive, and the long-term energy savings are not enough to offset the other more important losses: local jobs and local flavor. Bakeries are a staple in the community, and the fresh food and much-needed jobs they provide local inhabitants are more important to America's Main Streets than innovation is.

I am all for local businesses building their presence online and using computers to streamline accounting, but let's leave baking to the people who know how to bake. There are some things computers just can't do, and one of these concerns is taste. Maintain the local flavor. A return to the local bakery is what will save America.

Glossary

abundant   (uh-BUN-dunt) *adjective* plentiful; in large quantities (page 14)

agrarian   (uh-GRAIR-ee-un) *adjective* relating to an agriculture-based society (page 7)

annex   (uh-NEKS) *verb* to add a territory into an already existing one (page 34)

barge   (BARJ) *noun* a long boat, usually with a flat bottom, used to carry goods (page 20)

canal   (kuh-NAL) *noun* a long, narrow, human-made waterway (page 20)

emigration   (eh-mih-GRAY-shun) *noun* the act of leaving one's country for another (page 24)

famine   (FA-min) *noun* extreme scarcity of food (page 24)

fossil fuel   (FAH-sul FYOOL) *noun* a nonrenewable resource such as oil, coal, or natural gas (page 14)

immigration   (ih-mih-GRAY-shun) *noun* the act of people coming to a new place to live (page 24)

imperialism (im-PEER-ee-uh-lih-zum) *noun* a policy or practice by which a country increases its power by gaining control over other areas of the world (page 39)

industrialization (in-DUS-tree-uh-ly-ZAY-shun) *noun* the introduction of manufacturing, business, and other productive economic activity into an area (page 13)

monopoly (muh-NAH-puh-lee) *noun* the sole control of a product or service (page 35)

nationalism (NA-shuh-nuh-lih-zum) *noun* pride in one's country and desire for its independence (page 39)

scarce (SKAIRS) *adjective* rare; in small quantities (page 14)

secede (sih-SEED) *verb* to withdraw from (page 32)

steam engine (STEEM EN-jin) *noun* a machine, such as a train, that uses steam as its main power source (page 13)

strike (STRIKE) *noun* a work stoppage (page 29)

tenement (TEH-neh-ment) *noun* a run-down building separated into rooms for residence (page 31)

textile (TEK-stile) *adjective* relating to cloth or fabric (page 9)

turbine (TER-bine) *noun* a machine that uses flowing fluid and a rotating center piece to produce power (page 13)

union (YOON-yun) *noun* a group of laborers that work together to accomplish certain goals (page 29)

Index